Assdeep in Wonder

Other books by Christopher Gudgeon

Fiction
Greetings from the Vodka Sea
Song of Kosovo

Non-fiction
An Unfinished Conversation
Out of the World
Consider the Fish
The Luck of the Draw
The Naked Truth

Humour
You're Not As Good As You Think You Are

Assdeep in Wonder

Poems by Christopher Gudgeon

Anvil Press | 2016

Anvil Press Publishers Inc.
P.O. Box 3008, Main Post Office
Vancouver, B.C. V6B 3X5 Canada
www.anvilpress.com

Library and Archives Canada Cataloguing in Publication

Gudgeon, Christopher, 1959-, author
        Assdeep in wonder / Christopher Gudgeon.

Poems.
ISBN 978-1-77214-052-1 (paperback)

        1. Title.

PS8613.U44A88 2016   C811'.54   C2016-901184-4

Printed and bound in Canada
Cover illustration by Marc Uhre
Author photo: Bathroom Selfie
Interior by HeimatHouse
Represented in Canada by Publishers Group Canada
Distributed by Raincoast Books

The publisher gratefully acknowledges the financial assistance of the Canada Council for the Arts, the Canada Book Fund, and the Province of British Columbia through the B.C. Arts Council and the Book Publishing Tax Credit.

Canada Council Conseil des Arts
for the Arts du Canada

BRITISH COLUMBIA
ARTS COUNCIL
An agency of the Province of British Columbia

Canadä

To Philly with love.

Acknowledgments

"Let's start small, my darling" originally appeared in *subTerrain*.

"Waiting for Our Lord God Jesus Christ in the Maple Leaf Lounge at the John G. Diefenbaker Airport in Saskatoon, Saskatchewan" and "bill bissett spells his name with capital letters" originally appeared in *Geist*.

"Magician" originally appeared in the film *The Trick with the Gun*.

"The Revelations of Donald Trump" originally appeared in *Sewer Lid*.

"Future Tops of America" originally appeared in *Fine Print*.

Contents

Let's start small, my darling . . .

Let's start small, like elephants,
who never pass second base
on a first date.

We have whole lives ahead
of us, my darling, let's pace
ourselves, measure

love out a teaspoon at a
time, ration it like water
on a lifeboat.

Don't expect too much from that
first kiss, but hold on, other
kisses will come

in time, or not; we have just
this moment, expectation
will smother this

moment as surely as our
memories will carve it in soap.
The contemplation

of these two hearts as one — that's
for children, old women and
elephants. We

must be harder on ourselves
start small, because great love stands
on tiny feet.

Drinking with Al Purdy at the Quinte Hotel

We are drinking, Al and I, at the Quinte
Hotel and he is one beer closer to death.

I watch the famous yellow flower wilt
and ask Al if it's a kind of sunflower.

He answers: "How the fuck would I know, I ain't
a florist," then takes a sip of beer.

When the barmaid comes back, Al clinks
her tray with his empty glass

He points
at the withered blossom then asks: "What kind of flower is that?"

The barmaid looks and shakes her head as she thinks:
"Yellow?"

Al nods then orders another round of drinks,
then looks at me, shrugs.

"There's your answer, son. The Quinte
girls are renowned for their botanical acumen."

Al laughs at his own joke, wipes his thin
lip on his sleeve; we drink to the health of the dying flower.

Marriage

Someone to make me cold porridge and scratch behind my ears,
To hum me halting lullabies as actuaries calculate my years.
Someone to sit across from me as I eat, or beside, or just near;
Our conversation: knives gossip across plates, lips kissing up beer.

A pension with shoes and functioning hips, that's what I require
Who stops me from smoking and is still wooed with a flower,
Whose memory of passions is eas'ly confused
With the actual passion, long since diffused.

We'll share the same doctor, to save ourselves time,
Whatever diseases are yours will be mine;
I'll spoon you in bed, to keep us both warm,
And I'll fart without warning, you'll hold your breath without scorn.

One time each year, to celebrate our lean vows,
We'll put on a do, and our friends, all enjoweled,
Will stuff on their suits, unfurl Arabesque skirts;
We'll it eat 'til we're tired, chat 'til it hurts.

One night when you wake, to find I am dying,
You'll cry as the ambulance takes its own damn sweet time,
You'll be stoic at my funeral, quite merry at my wake,
And come home to our same house, not as empty as you'd like.

Yet I'll remain, some appendage of yours,
No one will mention your name without remembering ours,
'Til enough time has passed and our unshatterable lens
Is replaced by a book club and bridge night with friends.

If I were a Canadian poet

If I were a Canadian poet
I would wear a jacket and tie to go
about my business.

                    I would be outwardly
harsh and cynical, to protect my thin
membrane of paper, the microscopic
vowels and consonants that are my enzymes.

I would complain about the price of beer.

If I were a Canadian poet
I wouldn't have children, only poems, because
poems, like children, do not feed, but unlike
children, do not eat;

                    I would have no pets
'cept spondees and little iambs, because
pets must be fed and brushed and bathed
while poems need nothing but darkness and a
walk around the block every now and then.

At Christmas, I would give poems — useless as
those other gifts, but non-returnable —
and when I came to visit, friends would dredge
dresser drawers for my poems, arrange
them on the coffee table haphazard
as if they'd always been there, ready for
any pentametric emergency.

If I were a Canadian poet
I would stay at home on Friday night
waiting for the CBC to call. I'd
answer on the fourth ring, pretending
to be out-of-breath, surprised anyone
would be calling. If it's a wrong number,
I'd hang up then compose a poem about phones,
dedicated to the Canada Council.

If I were a Canadian poet
I would sell brushes door-to-door, I would
excavate ditches, I would try to sell
insurance over the phone, I would nurse
a cold to near-death and use up all my
sick days; I would be my patron, me and
UIC.

And when I got a grant, the oceans would
part, the heavens would part as well and word
like pure water would flow from my fingers
and word would become line (line, verse; verse, stanza).
Other poets would stink with envy
fearing there were no good words left.

If I were a Canadian poet
I would cultivate two memories:
One short, for insults,
the other long,
                    for expectation.

Sonnet for the Portuguese

There is precision to your indifference,
your housewife fingers stop my shoulders as
you lift your legs to draw me further in.
"Love is large," you say, kicking the flowered
sheets to the floor. What you mean, *dona*, is
that love is a trap. Blood red hibiscus,
yellow savannah flowers wilt at our
feet; I squeeze harder. There're other lovers
waiting by the door; but I've memorized
a poem — *cabe no breve espaco
de beijar*; as I tense the cord 'round your
wrists, you stop struggling. You love that I can
translate this language, but hate that, when I
push you to the bed, you fall so gently.

Talking to Alistair MacLeod about the death of Paul Quarrington

Nothing about us is right; nothing. The
fit of the shoes, the crooked taper of
the shirt, the cuffs chafing our thumb-bones,
loose pants hitched with tight belts. We'd make poor men
in ancient times, slave-tutors to a small prince,
unemployable bards, slim foragers;
in war, first to die, killed by friendly spear
or run through, suspended as we outthink
our escapes. Not even our widows would miss us.

He'd have made a shite caveman, we agree,
despite the Cromagnid ridge. He couldn't hunt
or gather, flint was not his medium.
He'd be good around a fire, though; he knew
where kindling hid, just when to blow the
embers; he could invent mythology
on the spot and answer big questions like:
how, in a world where death exceeds life at
every tick, guys like us ever survived?

Laureen Harper stung by a bee at a photo op on the roof of the Royal York Hotel, July 27, 2014.

1. Worker Bees

It's not true
that when a hon-
ey bee stings she dies,

she dies a
thousand times in
her brief life, every

flower breaks
her heart, every
pistil, every stamen:

they use you
once then never
call again. The larvae

are selfish
they take and take
and give nothing in

return, un-
grateful offspring
gorged on honey

with faces
that only a
Queen could love.

She's barren,
the worker bee,
and when she dances

she does so
with dignity and
a trace of sadness

that is lost
on the drones. The
other workers follow

her lead, mem–
orize the dance
and replicate it

ten thousand
times in their minds'
multi-lensed eye, then

dance themselves;
not out of in–
stinct, as one would think

but out of
spite and a mis–
placed sense of duty.

II. The Prime Minister Issues a Statement

A serious security breach
the investigation is underway
the head of CSIS personally checked the guest list
the honey bee is not on it
the bee hasn't been issued a press pass
the police interview eyewitnesses
the forensic artist completes a composite drawing
female
brown
approx. 12 millimetres in length
average build
prominent mandible
telltale proboscis
possibly used for drawing nectar from
a flower's heart

CSIS believes the bee is acting independently
a rogue bee
not part of a terrorist cell
or Jihadist network
al-Qaeda
al-Shabaab
Hamas
ISIS
the Armed Islamic Group of Algeria
she lay in wait concealed in
patio stones or a
flower pot
a cagey bitch if
ever there was one

the press is at a loss
they can't think of a clever name
to call the bee
an ingenious headline
it seems so simple
but nothing comes to mind

the Prime Minister issues a statement
a video message for his Facebook followers
he calls for calm and public order
bees in general are peaceable creatures
law abiding
bees are not anarchists
bees are hard-working, measured
they do not sting unless incited
an unhappy accident
we can learn from it
and grow
Laureen is shaken but recovering
she thanks you for your well-wishes
your thoughts, your prayers
the cards the
email messages have
helped us through this
difficult time

the Prime Minister pauses
his eyes well up
he can't find the words
he brings his hand to his mandible and

for a moment we
are reminded that
even he
is human.

III. Drones

flying gangbang cluster-fuck
mid-air orgy let's congregate
copulate propagate inseminate
bang that bitch bee queen cum-dump
she's a virgin after all
take her to heaven and back
forty times she can take it she
loves to feel bee cock deep in her honey pot
loves to get her bee-gina all sticky with bee jizz
talk about your royal jelly
make her moan you dirty drone bastards
she won't ask your name
she doesn't want to know you
she wants to fuck you senseless
then forget you ever met
for you she's the perfect score
the tight bee-atch   tight!
you tapped that bee-atch's bee-ass   tight!
for her an endless fuckfest
interchangeable distractions
loved in the moment and
forgotten the instant she
creams and
rips your cock off

IV. Photo Op

"Ok, Mrs. Harper
we'd like one more
with the bee."

V. The Queens

Bees are dying,
hives are disappearing,
not one at a time;
all at once.
The queens held council;
are giving up being bees,
they'd rather be Mayflies
or cicadas.
Other species are joining in.
Pilot whales have run aground on the beaches
of Okinawa, the Faeroe Islands, Martha's Vineyard
stranded in the sand
like so many vacationed Kennedys.
Siberian tigers are slashing their wrists,
lengthwise,
tired of near-extinction,
the unnecessary pressure.
Red pandas are no longer eating
ingesting only black coffee and clear liquids;
they take no visitors.
Leatherbacks, skipjacks, and poison dart frogs
have signed suicide pacts,
voiding their insurance policies.
narwhales, jaguars, and southern rock-hopper penguins
have formed support groups;
to no avail,
no one feels supported.
Black rhinos contemplate how things would be different
if only they'd had antlers instead of horns;
they skip town in the middle of the night
without leaving any forwarding addresses.
Even the rats are feeling the heat,

they talk of packing it in,
moving back to Norway;
you can be vermin for only so long
before it starts to get you down.
Still, the lemmings are happy,
crying "I told you so" as they leap
to their deaths.

Lemmings love it when they're right.

bpNichol dancing with a swan

I am   d a ^{n} c ^{i} n g   with $^{\cap}_{\substack{O\\\lambda}}$

       (AND IT'S AS IF)

I am $_d$ a ^{n} c ^{i} $_n$ ^{g} with a

       ƨwɒⁿ

Sonnet written in a bathhouse

For Niklas

There is a lunacy to the dark, how
an ass this soft makes me so hard, this
perfect stalls me with imperfection. The
waning light reveals: even though I can
never fill you, I can leave you empty.
I taste the tea on your lips, wonder:
can I spread you far enough apart, fit
it all inside? The better parts: my cock,
my back, the reptile brain, every hair,
each heartbeat, the lonely, lovely sorrows?
There is small gravity inside you; I
spring across your moonscape, pin your wrists
above the bed. You bite my chin and we
celebrate a darkness colder than love.

Codependence

naked in the sea
the riptide tears at our skin
as we become pearls

Waiting for Our Lord God Jesus Christ in the Maple Leaf Lounge at the John G. Diefenbaker Airport in Saskatoon, Saskatchewan

Assdeep in chair, Molsoned, enGlobed, my hands
Purelled clean, my heart unfribulating.
I touch nothing.

My hands are clean, I have washed myself of
it: the dirty thing that cannot been seen.
Prokaryotic microorganism,
that invisible thing that makes me shit
unwinding, violent rivers of shit,
praying to God in Marriot bathrooms
when I would rather be meeting with the
western reps in Milwaukee or Scottsdale
or Denver or Calgary, when I would
rather stand in the buffet line
at the Hilton President, Kansas City,
contemplating a Western omelet, when
I would rather be waiting for Our Lord
God Jesus Christ in the Maple Leaf Lounge
at the John G. Diefenbaker Airport
in Saskatoon, Saskatchewan.
Lord Jesus Christ, Son of God, have mercy
on me, a sinner. My hands are clean.
I touch nothing.

We have taken a vow of silence here
in the Maple Leaf Lounge at the John G.
Diefenbaker Airport in Saskatoon,

Saskatchewan. Our phones are on mute and
if we speak it is only to the Choirs
Angelic, invisible, dwelling in
the air: we praise the Seraphim,
as they cluster round our holy seats,
scrubbed vinyl discomforts, impossible
for sleep, possible for contemplation.
We sing their praises, the Seraphim; they
praise us back, singing "Holy, Holy
Holy is the Lord of Hosts! He fills this
lounge with His glory." We praise the four-
faced Cherubim, Man and Lion and
Accountant and Celebrity Chef. We praise
the just Erelim, perfect wheels within wheels,
we praise the Hashmallim, the Stongholds, the
Exousiai, submitting ourselves to their
physics, the mechanic workings of
gravity, time, electricity and
kerosene that govern the world beyond
the Maple Leaf Lounge at the John G.
Diefenbaker Airport in Saskatoon,
Saskatchewan. We praise the Princes, seek
their blessings, we praise the Heralds, the
Archangels, the Angels, we whisper their
names and write hallelujah in our cross-
word books.

          Mostly, we are celibate,
obedient; we have eschewed material comfort
and want for nothing. God watches over us: He
is delicious and savoury; He is
a slice of Kraft Cheddar or Edam, He
is a saltine and a Pringle and a
package of trail mix. This beer is His blood.
We're surrounded by sacrament, assdeep

in the wonder of His works. And when we
rise above the clouds, we promise to not
look down on Him in His heaven, instead,
we will memorize the location of the
nearest exits, keep our tables
and trays upright and in the locked
position for take-off and landing. There is
a woman amongst us. She is looking
at her cell phone, she is weeping.
Has she been bumped? We dare not
think. We do not look at one another.
Lord Jesus Christ, Son of God, have mercy on
us, we are sinners. But, our hands are clean.
We touch nothing.

There are other martyrs in the Maple
Leaf Lounge at the John G. Diefenbaker
Airport in Saskatoon, Saskatchewan.
The bumped and unaeroplanned, the old men
and women whose baggage exceeds their
carry-on allowances. We do not
look at them. They are in God's hands now. We
look instead outside the window, past the
iron birds, the metal angels, to the aspen parklands,
Martensville, Prince Albert, North Battleford,
past the tea-totaled boundaries set
by the Temperance Colonization
Society, devoted to sober
industry and land speculation, from
Clark's Crossing to Moose Woods; we look beyond
to the graves of frozen Indians, Chief Rain-
in-the-Face, Big Wampum, Running Bear
and Tonto, naked graves for the frozen smiling
heathens, Rod Naistus, Larry Wegner, Neil

Stonechild, cold happy martyrs, tourists,
frozen in time, reminding us that all things
come to those who wait, especially if
what they are waiting for is death.

                                        Inside
the Maple Leaf Lounge at the John G.
Diefenbaker Airport in Saskatoon,
Saskatchewan, we are warm, time is unfrozen.
The pilots enter with their yoga mats
and lead us through. Utkatasana, The Awkward
Chair Pose; Svarga Dvidasana, the Bird
of Paradise Pose; the Cow Face Pose,
Gomukhasana; everything but the
Airplane Pose, which has no name, and if it
did, could not be uttered. We breathe in
relaxation, breathe out tension, just like God
and the hypnotherapists tell us; we
contemplate the idea of God as Pilot
and consider the mystic name of
Jesus as revealed by the Kabbalists
Isaac the Blind, Madonna Ciccone
Penn Richie. Yeshua, Lord Jesus Christ,
Son of God, have mercy on us, we are
sinners. Wash us in your grace.
                                        Touch us.

Inside the Maple Leaf Lounge at the John
G. Diefenbaker Airport in Saskatoon,
Saskatchewan, I check the departure screen,
I reread my boarding pass. Heather will
call my row number soon, and I will think
of her husband Roy back in Winnipeg,
who does or does not have lung cancer (the

doctors are not yet sure). Time is running
out. I want to be forgiven, but I
am comfortable. I want to wash in
Your grace, but the incoming passengers
are already deplaning. I will cleanse my
hands again, destroying microscopic
connections, wait for my turn to stow my
carry-on luggage safely on the floor
under the seat in front of me or in
the nearest available over-head
compartment. When the rapture comes, Lord
Jesus Christ, Son of God, to the Maple
Leaf Lounge at the John G. Diefenbaker
Airport in Saskatoon, Saskatchewan,
have mercy on me, a sinner, for I have
listened to the pronouncements, have
restricted gels and liquids, have snapped my
safety belt, I have ensured — Hallelujah! —
that my seat is in the full upright position,
I have promised that, in the unlikely
event of a loss of cabin pressure, I
will place the oxygen mask over my
mouth and nose, will breath normally, and,
if I am traveling with a small child,
will secure my mask first, then help
the child secure hers. And so we wait as the
pimpled security guard checks his iPhone,
wipes his hand on his shirt sleeve
and tries to stifle a yawn
as he wishes
he was anywhere
but here.

The good father

we couldn't father him
he was too much child for any of us
so we arranged him
embalmed him in our hate

a decorative corpse
that could hurt you
if it toppled over
but was otherwise harmless

decomposing at our leisure
unable to scratch
at the coffin boards
or tap out an SOS with his eyes

he didn't have to play dead
because we killed him
and no one noticed he was missing
except when he was there

The Causes of Heterosexuality

Scientists have looked, but cannot find,
the biochemical factors that underlie
heterosexual attraction — the epigenetic line
that drives these behaviours, makes a girl and a guy
shed their clothes then, breathless, hesitate
before they lunge to procreate.
Perhaps, it's thought, a mutant gene
has disrupted what could have been
or maybe it's an environmental thing —
some suggest, a reserved mother
with measured love, who did not smother
or a not-distant father, warm, attending
who forced out the offspring's latent need
to find a boy or girl and breed.

This behaviour's been observed in several species
the polecat, American bison, mallard duck
and all sorts of primates, bonobos, rhesus
after a couple drinks, they'll pair off to fuck;
even fruitflies and the occasional gnat
after a kiss with some tongue, will take off their pants.
No one can explain these aberrant proclivities
despite the grants and research activities;
what compels the two sexes of one kind
to defy biology, good taste and natural law?
Is it an inherent weakness? A character flaw?
Scientists can't say, there's no markers, no signs;
but they'll figure it out one day, I am sure,
then they can focus our efforts on finding a cure.

hanging raymond souster out to dry

i went to visit the poet raymond souster to
talk about poetry and the poet milton acorn
but souster wouldn't let me in because he said
he was sick so i stood outside and talked to him
through the intercom.

i told this story to the poet al purdy who said
that the poet raymond souster was shy and a
bit of an oddball and that his wife was crazy
and that's why souster didn't let people into
his house; besides, al said, souster wasn't a
good poet anyhow.

i told the poet bill howell what the poet al purdy
said and bill told me how he visited the poet
raymond souster once, how he did go into
souster's house; he found souster in the basement
frantically hanging drafts of old poems and letters
on a clothesline because a pipe'd burst and all these
papers got wet.

bill figured maybe souster was worried about
his literary legacy, protecting his stuff so future
generations could also not give a shit, so bill asked:
'ray, why bother?' and souster, on the verge of tears
said that the university of toronto wanted his archives
and was willing to pay good money. 'wet, my life is
worth nothing at all, bill, but dry — dry — it has value
by the inch.'

Make Room in Your Life for Me

Make room in your life for me, my own true:
unkiss all the kisses that we didn't do,
unlove all the lovers that you loved before,
unvow all the vows, unwhore all the whores,
I'll unmake the mistakes that were made without you,
You'll unoth all the others, undo all the do.

Make room in your bed, my sweet sleepy bairn:
scooch to one side, rest your head on my arm,
the cat, she can sleep in a box on the floor,
and we'll bury all your sex toys away in a drawer,
I'm batteries-included, work like a charm,
and on cold nights I will cover you, keep your toes warm.

Make room at your table, my handsome young brother:
we'll set just one setting, can sit with each other,
two chair's one too many, our bums, they can share;
we don't need a plate or fine silverware;
we'll get Chinese food from a place we'll discover
one chopstick each, for you and your lover.

Make room for me in your tub, my wat'ry soul mate,
my two lips can scour you and exfoliate;
the ducky can go, cast the luffa aside,
I'll scrub all those places your fingers can't find,
I'll discover each blackhead, then obliterate
as your water bill drops at a remarkable rate.

Make room in your garden, my not-taken-for-granted:
pull out snapdragon, red amaranthes,
tear up the lavender, narcissus, yellow peony,

destroy *Dianthus barbatus*, babies' breath, every begony,
we'll supplant every plant your old lovers planted,
who knew a dead garden could be so romantic?

Make room in your heart, my unhummable hum:
you don't need all those ventricles, aorta, atrium;
I'll regulate flow from your toes to your head,
make your heart skip a beat when my name is said,
I'll pump slow when you stroll, fast when you run
and engorge the engorgeous when we get it on.

So make us some room, my untamable you:
unoth all the others, undo all the do,
I will become your enduring distraction
and even in death we'll sustain the attraction,
compactly compacted we'll decompose, I and you,
forever interred in a coffin for two.

He loves me...

If this flower was
a hand, a fist, and within
this fist, this flower,
was a secret, could you strip
the petals off to

see inside? It relaxes,
this fist, as the sun
rises, and is business for
only bees and breeze
'til the sober moon

settles. Could you strike me with
this flower? Grab my throat with
it while you push me
to my knees, tell me — hush;
everything will be

okay? As I tear each
finger from the peduncle —
he loves me, he loves
me not — will I see something
familiar in your

daisy eye? Will I have time to
brace myself before the
flower stoops to tell me —
hush, my love; it's time
for sleep? It's just a

flower, and flowers, like secrets,
cannot hurt
you, and, like fists, only
close to protect themselves
from the night.

Dave McFadden's Truth Machine

truthstruthtruthstruthstruthtruthstruthstruthstruth
truthstruthtruthstruthtruthstruthtruthstruthstruths
truthstruthstruthtruthliestruthtruthstruthtruthslies
truthstruthtruthslietruthtruthsliestruthstruthslielies
truthtruthtruthstruthstruthstruthtruthstruthstruths
truthstruthstruthsliestruthstruthsliethruthstruthslies
truthstruthsliestruthstruthstruthstruthsliestruthlies
truthsliestruthliestruthstruthsliesliestruthstruthslies
lietruththruthliesthruthliesthruthliestruthsliestruths
liestruththruthsliestruthsthruthlietruthslieliestruths
truthstruthsliesliestruthstruthstruthsliestruthstruths
liesliestruthsliestruthsthruthsliesliesliestruthslies
lielieliesliestruthliesliesliesliestruthsliesliestruthslies
liestruthliesliesliesliethruthslieslieslielieslieslieslie
lieslielieslieslieslieliesliesslieliestruthliesliesliesslies
lieslielieliesliesliesslieliesliesliesliesliesslieliesslieslies

The last generation

proper children
in white dress shirts
Oxford knot
lipstick lifted
from mother's clutch
wait for Easter to pass
she stretches her toes
on a coarse blanket
adjusts her elbow
scratches her initials
on the bed post
he chases a wood bug
into a paper cup
they have no middle
the proper children
only edges
mother's always said this

the proper boy
guards the door at night
rides his hobby horse
into that black place
raises his toy gun
to the darkness
takes aim at
father's soft heart
the proper girl
stretches her toes
in the cold sheets
listens as summer rots
under the floorboards

the proper girl
removes her shirt
waits for mother
to drink her tea
waits for father
to finish reading the
sad news of the day
the proper boy
undoes the Oxford knot
cracks the bunny's chocolate ear
they have no middle
the proper children
not the lost generation
but the last
and they shall live and live
in places adjusted
for their comfort

amphetaminedays

i wish for binary this and that with all the
               gaps   plugged by chemical distraction

we have our genders manandwoman   our
          sockets aligned manintowoman   as the engineers

intended   pharmacists connect us to propriety

               but

as *lisdexamfetamine dimesylate* bonds with   unproper

it's   ungendered grammars that can't conceal a lack
of preference   thisandthatbodyandmindmanandwoman

onesex   nuance is nuisance girlboy   but
drug or no drug   i'm gonna get in-side you   and

                              metabolize

Codependence

i.
she said she'd jack me off if I got her some coke
I said if she'd blow me I'd see what I could do

I bought a few lines from a skater at Keele Station
she gave me the worst head I'd had in my life

ii.
he was still high when he called from the bus
I said to come over but that he couldn't stay

he smoked a roach that he found in the yard
I let him pass out at the end of the bed

iii.
she wanted to watch him get fucked from behind
I said I would do it if she played with herself

she made him wear lipstick and called him a faggot
I pinched his soft skin 'til he started to cry

iv.
he needed sixty bucks for two tabs of acid
I said that I never paid to have sex

he let me fuck him 'cause he couldn't get high
I gave him three twenties to take a cab home

v.
she liked to come over get pissed on the couch
I'd stay up all night making Black Russians

she wanted to hold me and pass out at sunrise
I wanted to cum one more time before sleep

Magician

There's an art to this deception, built on
distraction and perspective. My magic depends
              on where you stand.

Nothing I do is honest. I offer you a
flower and pull a dove instead from that
              secret place.

The truth is, it's all done with wires
and shadow and a terrible sincerity that
              passes for love.

It doesn't matter that death still waits, hiding
its rabbits in all those false bottoms.
              What matters is:

even though it's all a lie, you need it to be
true; even though I can't be trusted,
              I need you to believe in me.

Canadian Tourister

Canada is an igloo melting in the sun.

Canada is a wolf-fur parka, hanging on an ice peg
outside of an igloo melting in the sun.

Canada is an Eskimo on a train, with her luggage at her feet,
following the sun as it sets in the west,
thinking of a wolf-fur parka at the door
of her igloo; she eats smoked Lake
Winnipeg goldeye, contemplating Indians
and the RCMP Musical Ride. She is
so far from home.

Canada is a salmon on life-support hidden in the suitcase
of the Eskimo on the train,
she is following the sun as it sets in the never-present west,
thinking of a wolf in fur parka at the door of her igloo
as she eats smoked Lake Winnipeg goldeye,
contemplates Red Indians and the RCMP Musical Ride, so far from home
repeating her mantra — tundra — 'til the word sticks to her lips
like a cherry popsicle in July heat.

She is a sheep in wolf-fur parka, an Edmonton Eskimo,
so far from home, following the
never-setting sun, contemplating golden-eyed gods,
the Musical Ride, rye-and-sevens and the Indians that stick to her lips
like a cherry popsicle on life-support.

Canada is a Cape Breton fiddler pausing to sip his rye-and-maple syrup.

The Cape Breton fiddler is on life-support and, thanks to
Tommy Douglas and Medicare,

hidden in the suitcase of an Eskimo on a train heading west or east
traversing the Rocky Mountains, as the Mounties in perfect formation
chase Sitting Bull to the Dakota boarder. He is so far from home.

Canada is a caribou. Canada is a moose. Canada is a black-tailed deer.
They are wandering. Navigating. Migrating. Concerned ungulates,
trying to make it to the border
before they wear out their welcome.
They are defining themselves in terms of others' expectations.
They are so far from home.

Canada is not a beaver. Canada is a beaver hat. It is a
salmon on life-support
hidden in the suitcase of the Eskimo on the train,
following the sun as it sets in the never-present west,
thinking of a wolf in fur parka at the door of her igloo
eating smoked prefab bannock,
contemplating Red Indians and the RCMP Musical Ride
repeating her mantra — tundra — 'til the word melts on her lips
like a cherry popsicle in July heat,
navigating,
migrating,
trying to make it to the border.
She has already worn out her welcome,
she has already defined herself in terms of others' expectations.

Canada is a hitchhiker on the Highway of Tears;
so far from home.

Canada is a Russian stripper, pressing her tits into the
face of a Japanese businessman as he slips twenty dollars
into her g-string. They are so lonely and
so far from home.
Canada is not North. That is a lie perpetrated
by Margaret Atwood.

Canada is nowhere and everywhere.
a White Nothing, a Red Everything.
Not a point on a compass,
all points on all compasses,
the magnetic north, south, east and west,
the unnatural loadstone.

Canada is a man-made lake.
A manufactured landscape.
A manufactured literature.
Canada is a navvie laying dynamite, swingin' his
hammer in the shitty morning sun. It is a Pinoy
boy working the graveyard at Timmy's
making Maple Dips and Old Fashioned Plains
who scalds his thumb
replacing the coffee filter.

Canada is a long, long poem about Canada.

Canada has no history books,
they are being written as we speak
by navvies and temporary foreign workers,
by strippers and hitchhikers
and runaways who star in post office posters.

Canada is a bag of warm milk, a plastic
udder left in the sun.
Even the cows are lonely, suckling mechanical calves,
no better or worse than other cows
just colder than most and
so far from home.
The Pope has stopped trying to define Canada. He stopped
praying for us when we stopped praying for him.
You have everything you need, he says, you don't need my help.

The Pope spins an ornate globe, made of alabaster and vellum
everywhere is Canada and not-Canada. Miracles he understands,
but not this.

Canada is a caribou on life-support
hidden in Tommy Douglas' suitcase,
packed in the back of a panel van
driving the 401, just outside Medicine Hat,
it is a Russian stripper
eating smoked Lake Winnipeg goldeye,
contemplating Red Indians and the RCMP Musical Ride
repeating her mantra — work permit — 'til the words, like hot wax, drip
from her lips.

We are whores of wood.
We are drawers of water-colour landscapes.

Canada is a businessman named Norman or Gord or something
working for CIBC or Rogers Telecom or something
in a suit he got from Moore's or Harry Rosen or someplace like that
having some beers after work in a strip club on
Yonge St.
Rue St. Catherine
Portage Ave.
texting his wife — Karen? Gail? — who's on a GO Train somewhere,
going home or something,
and he's telling her he'll be home soon: as he waves the
girl over for one more
lap dance.

Canada is a bouquet of wildflowers,
blazing stars, bloodroots,
wild yellow lily and evening primrose,
rotting on the side of Highway 16

just east of Rupert,
it's a bouquet of names
Delphine Nikal,
Ramona Wilson,
Tamara Chipman,
Shelly Ann Bascu,
left at the side of the road,
migrating names,
no longer moving,
no longer alone,
so far from home.

Canada is a peacekeeper's bullet,
a priest's love child,
a barren cow, a moose calf learning to walk
on ice.

Canada is a temporary worker on life support.
The oxygen tank wheezes as he flips the meat patty and
unwraps a slice of Kraft processed cheese;
he's hidden, like a salmon in a suitcase,
underneath the floorboards,
dreaming of the ever-expanding continent,
thinking of a woman in faux fur,
sipping her double-double as she licks her lips
and contemplates getting a stripper pole installed
in the rec room, because that's a good workout,
repeating her mantra — core — 'til the word melts,
leaving her lips
the colour of cherry popsicles.
She is navigating.
She is migrating.
She is trying to digest
everything.

She does not know where her border is.
She has never had to find her border.
She will never wear out her welcome.
She understands that she only exists in the minds of others,
and that makes her happy.
Sometimes she is lonely and always
she is so far from home.

Canada is a caribou on life-support
hidden in Tommy Douglas' suitcase,
packed in the back of a panel van
driving the Trans Canada just outside Medicine Hat
driving Highway 16 east of Prince George
driving No. 4 through Big Pond,
looking for the tell-tale igloo,7
looking for the wolves at the door,
it is a Russian stripper
eating smoked Lake Winnipeg goldeye and bannock,
contemplating Red Indians and the RCMP Musical Ride,
repeating her mantra — work permit — 'til the word melts on her lips
trying to make it to the border
before she wears out her visa;
she cinches the housecoat around her waist, blows a kiss
to the businessman nursing a pair of rye-and-cokes
who takes a sip and says to no one in particular:
she is like a poem or a twenty-dollar bill,
she is like a landscape painting of the tundra,
she's the most beautiful thing I've ever seen,
she's so, so lonely and so, so very far from home.

Talking to Paul Quarrington about the death of Alistair MacLeod (after we rescued a stripper from drowning)

There is a true
story about the
the night after
MacLeod died and
Paul and I went
to Grenadier
Pond for no good
reason and how,
after toasting
Al MacLeod, we
found a woman
— a stripper from
Russia — in the
water in just her
underwear and
socks. Paul found a
blanket somewheres
and a thermos
full of Irish
coffee somewheres
else; the Russian
stripper told us
the cops took her
daughter away
and that's why she
wanted to die.
Paul nodded and
said nothing, which
was the perfect

thing to say. Soon
other people
came over and
wanted to know
what happened, and
we huddled in
close to keep warm
and somehow the
conversation
came around to
Anton Chekhov's
*Lady With the
Dog*; the stripper
recited a long
passage from
memory and
we almost cried
because the words
sounded more
beautiful in
Chekhov's native
language. Soon
the ambulance
came to take the
Russian lady
away, but none
of us wanted
to leave, least of
all Paul, so we
lingered to drink
to the mem'ry
of Alistair
MacLeod and to
the happiness

of the woman
we'd pulled from
Grenadier Pond
and one more toast
to the health of
the late Carlos
Montenegro,
hero of Paul's
unfinished book,
Dead to Rights. And
then we drank to
our own health and
then we just drank.
Finally, when
everyone'd left,
Paul discovered
some rum in his
pockets, then we
tried to climb the
icy hill in our
dress shoes, until
Paul gave up, sat
on a park bench
and, pouring one
more drink, said: "I
wish MacLeod was
here; this is the
kind of shit he
loved." Then Paul
found a cigar
in his jacket,
lit it, took a
long drag and said:
"There are cultures

where we'd be
kinda married,
the stripper and
I, because of
all the things we
did; although, we
are married in
a different
kind of way, I
suppose, because
of all the things
that we didn't do."

Siege

You built a rampart with my affection
to keep out Turks and Mongol hordes;
and if I ever caught you unshuttered,
I'd reach my dirty fingers through the
slats, caress before you drew up again.
I retreated, not wounded; your fortress
was cool but had smooth edges. Now
the walls are tender, ma; the hoardings
have long rotted. I see you peek through
the crenels, unplot my tactics, consider
capitulation. No Orientals wait to breech
your walls; just me, curious tourist, who
comes on Christmas Day to have his photo
taken, a picture to keep on the fridge door,
measure your decay. I won't slip my finger
through, to scratch at the bolt; instead, I'll
consider this monument, eroded by its own
grit, then tip my cheek against the gate, as
you press your shoulder to the other side,
bend your one good knee, and push back.

Come, Let Us Bathe Milton Acorn!

Come, let us bathe Milton
Acorn in rosewater and
red wine, let us rub him
with fine oils and perfumed
rags, decorate his hair
with the feathers of eagles
and smaller less-serious
birds. Let us gild his
hemorrhoids and paint
his liver spots every colour
of the rainbow. Let us wash
his clothes in bleach and
strong detergent, festoon
his coat with ribbons and
coffee stains. Let us buy him a
real belt with notches, not
fashioned with scissors and
a phillip's screwdriver, but factory
installed, like a new car smell.
Shall we carry him through
the traffic on carpets made of
horsehair and fine cardboard?
The sun will surely groan with
wonder and everyone we pass
will ask: is that a poet or merely
some glorious human cigar?

The Fruit Machine

Sexual abnormalities appear to be the favourite target of hostile intelligence agencies, and…the nature of homosexuality appears to adapt itself to this kind of exploitation.
        —excerpt from a 1959 memo to the Canadian Security Panel

i. Word Association

Flower?
Penis.

Dog?
Penis.

Ensconce?
Penis.

Infiltrate?
Rectum. No, wait; penis.

Black?
Penis!

Sanctuary?
Penis.

Intercourse?
Between two courses.

Sodomy?
Sodom-you.

Just kidding:
Penis.

ii. Galvanic Skin Response

The images:
a daffodil;
a Persian cat
with a ball of
yellow yarn; a
tanned boy in
tennis whites,
leans over the
net to return
a volley; a
family picnic,
the mother, in
a sun dress, the
colour of lime
Freshie, spreads
margarine on a
cracker as the
red-haired daughter
in a checkerboard
two-piece, lies
on her stomach
and struggles to
open a jar of
raspberry jam;
an oiled body-
builder in a
tight posing pouch,
holds this plastic
Earth on his back;
stiletto heels
— black — set in a
nest of crimson

59

velvet; acned
lady, frozen
mid-blink, two cocks
in her mouth, one
black, the other
white.

You want to ask,
"Who selected these pictures?
I mean, surely they say
more about him than
they do about
me."

iii. Pupillary Response Test

Electronic coonhound
or Belgian Shepherd
can detect
a single drop of gay
in a summer lake
of straight,
a trace of faggot residue
concealed but uneradicable
like an indiscretion
in the eyes of God.

A single particle of faggot
can hang in the air for seventeen hours.
When it wafts
down-wind
the dog lifts its nose
shows its teeth.
The fruit machine

better than your auntie's gaydar,
built by serious men
calibrating
electronic resistance,
vacuum tubes,
apertures set.
You are strapped in place,
arms, wrists
secure,
head
secure,
immobilized,
you are
completely submissive
technology's bitch
power bottom to the nation.

The safe word is "Diefenbaker."

poemdictatedbytheghostofmichaelondaatje

theresatrick
withapoem
thatimlearn
ingtheresa
trickwitha
poemthatim
theresatrick
withapoem
thatimlearn
ingtheresa
trickwitha
poemthatim
learningto
dotheresa
trickwitha
poemthatim
learningto
theresatrick
theresatrick
withaghost
thatimpoem
ingtolearn
withaghost
withaghost
theresatrick
theresapoem
withaknife
withaknife
withaknife
thatimlearn
ingtothat
imlearning
todomichael

unchristmas

this distance
in the air
(snow angels in the gravel)

frozen breaths hang
peppermint lip gloss
inverted like St. Peter's cross
(unlikely and as terrible)
we celebrate unchristmas
in our various rooms

contemplate our nativity

(baby Jesus rogers a lamb)
(wise kings marvel at a
marshmallow elf)

wait

forgotten lovers remember'd

gift 1: iPhone
gift 2: Facebook

delete your number
remove your pictures
erase those parts of the year

already lost
carol (bel canto)
as memories

"This is not the time of love."
slither round your neck

breath

bill bissett spells his name with capital letters

it happens on saturday evening
after the stray dogs in stanley park have
eaten their supper and before the canada
geese have fallen asleep in the lagoon:
bill bissett spells his name with capital letters;

the dogs are not impressed, their teeth are
uppercase, the wind carries their grammar
the wind is their verb and their noun — they
don't need predicate, adjective,
adverb, conjunction; they piss in first person singular
each drop a golden monograph on the
handkerchief-earth;

nor are the canada geese impressed when
bill bissett spells his name with capital letters;
the geese are asleep, their heads tucked under
their wings (geese dream only apostrophe
and comma); they *are* impressed bill bissett
writes in pencil first, because when geese will
write they are certain they will write in
pencil only (geese always look forward
to erasing their next mistake);

bill bissett spells his name with capital
letters finally in ink, without looking,
for the capital, once seen — like the word
once uttered and heard, if only by a
goose or a poet — can't be retracted.
bill bissett is cautious;

he sees that capital letters begin
every sentence but end none and, while
every thing has many names,
few of them are proper.

do not feed the bear

you'll make a tasty morse
l kitten, and as much as yo
u want me to gnaw you ra
w from the bone, I'm not t
he animal l once was. I'm
near-sighted, dear, my bac
k hurts; your beauty narro
ws my resolve. I'll eat you
proper, with a knife & fork.

you think it's a jungle in m
y bed, kitty, but l must gua
rd my tame heart, must stop
my easy fingers from quiver
ing; even as l crimp my lips
and display my canine teeth
, you already see: I'm an in
efficient predator, love, alm
ost alone, very near satiable.

Codependence

Come lay with me in my second best bed,
make it better with the sweetness of your quiet.
I'll furl the pillows 'round our heads,
and hoist up a towel to dampen the light.
Imagine we sail on that crystalline boat,
together 'xplore our more temperate waters,
our breaths, the spice winds, take meandering routes.
We'll anchor the headboard under tropical stars.
I'll brush the ashes from your hair,
cling to you through those semaphore fits,
as you drift into methodical sleep. It's there
I'll wait, counting heartbeats 'til the sun lifts.
When we awake we'll claw at the fetters,
promise ourselves, today'll be better.

The Revelations of Donald Trump

I am living vicariously through my own lives,
all of them, all at once, learning, living, loving,
projecting myself, being projected,
broadcasting for the End of Times,
setting things in motion,
putting myself out there via
super high frequency radio waves,
mobile broadband, broadcasting from
the tallest buildings —
Burj Khalifa,
Makkah Royal Clock Tower Hotel,
One World Trade Centre,
Taipei 101 —
to everyone, everywhere, all at once,
ever-vital, like a spider, youthy, open to all possibilities,
youngish, because fifty is the new thirty, sombre as a book,
I connect through devices hardwired into coffee shop countertops
and kindergarten desks, America,
through devices mounted on bus station walls, beside ads for
instant cash loans and pre-approved life insurance,
America, no questions asked; I project my visage onto billboards
in Decatur and Baton Rouge
and Inuvik and Kuwait City,
onto billboards in Johannesburg and Baden-Baden,
billboards shining down on the Battlefield of Kurukshetra,
where the ghosts of warriors shiver under the mute moon,
the Plains of Abraham, where the ghosts of warriors shiver
under the mute moon, the Field of Blackbirds,
where the ghosts of warriors drink plum wine and shiver
under the mute moon, electronic billboards shining
down on the fields of Choeung Ek, where there are no warriors,
only silence and the promise of flowers, billboards —

digital, pixilated, like quiet stars — shining
down on mud huts and cardboard shelters in Washington, DC,
Mexico City, on frozen bus shelters in Ottawa, Ontario, on clapboard
shanties in Shanghai and high-occupancy dumpsters
in every corner of this cornerless globe, because there are
no corners in America; I connect through microchips implanted
in the cerebral cortex of wild dogs and homeless men, who howl
at the freezing air then bark at Jesus Christ Himself, (infected,
like the rest of us, by his own glory, shining down, like the rest of us,
self-illuminated, five million pixels at a time),
I connect through digital receptors, America, injected into the
cerebellum of white rats, caged in cosmetics labs, drunk on
Revlon Colorstay Eyeliner, tripping on Este Lauder Pure Color Envy
Sculpting Lipstick, receptors implanted into the pituitary glands
of Guantanamo detainees, old men now, undressed of youth
and loaned out to the Body Shop, Lululemon and a rash of
pharmaceutical companies, to test facial scrubs, infused teas,
penile implants, stain-resistant yoga mats; connecting through digital
receptors surgically inserted into the spinal cords of untouchables —
Dalits and Burakumin; Cagots and Ragyabpa; wetbacks and the
working poor, minimum wage earners, homo sacers and homo
sexuals and unemployed homunculi and anyone else who is
harshing my buzz...

I am time grown old, America,
I am creating world destruction, America,
living vicariously through my own lives,
projecting myself in Möbius selfies,
the image of the image of the image of me,
a small god with big hair,
as I rend my vestments, turn in on myself,
yinning my yang,
autosarcophagic,
devouring myself a cell at a time,
then shitting myself out in great magic heaps

that digitalize and disperse,
that collect and reconnect and leave an imprint in my mind
of the image of the image of the image of the image;
I am reproducing strategically, America,
heterogamously,
as the mood suits me,
spraying my seed casually, like insecticide, as the mood
suits me, polysexual, not at all binary, lascivious as Solomon's
pomegranate, fucking without
issue, just for the pleasure of pleasing
myself as you
watch me please you,
and then, at once,
splitting myself into a thousand fragments,
each cluster of gemma
is potential,
each cluster
broadcasting my gene code,
dividing myself into a thousand new selves,
ever youthful,
all of them, learning, living, loving,
all of them projecting and being projected,
putting themselves out there
as I stand to the side of the frame,
staring into the bathroom mirror — five million pixels worth,
five million points of light — underwear to my knees, cock,
hard, photo ready, fist pumping, one more selfie, one more
dick pic for the road; I listen through my headphones,
as I sing a song to myself, my almost naked
self,
sing a song
celebrating myself,
a song
in praise of
myself,

hosanna to me
as Whitman hugs his bedfellow
and deciphers the poetry of the stars,
I sing myself into being,
a hymn to me — Oh praise be to me on high! —
and I say unto me, as certain as the Prophets — Ezekiel, Ibrahim,
Samuel, Hubbard — sang the songs of themselves,
lamented themselves into being,
I too sing, America,
because, like you, America, I am everywhere and all things, and
like you, I have come to set things in motion,
I too sing because I am meter and rhyme, America;
I too sing because I am melody, auto-tuned, sung by me,
about me, to me,
in perfect pitch,
counterpoint to my counterpoint,
contradictory, harmonious yet unresolved,
ever modulating:
my song is available on iTunes and Amazon the moment I intone it;
Oprah has it on her iPod,
and — man! — she can't get enough...

I am dazzled by the sun as it rises, America,
countless pixels, America,
I am strapped to the ground by the sun as it
scrapes across the morning;
I am chained every morning to the ground by the sun
it hurts my teeth as it squeaks across the sky
broadcasting itself,
the arrogant sun,
the cancerous sun,
ten thousand degrees Fahrenheit,
casting shadows across the Book of the Dead,
the Book for the End of Times and the other books all unopened,
un-cut, unread, still writing themselves in reverse, a kind of unwriting

that is in itself
a kind of writing, the cancerous
sun, melting the icecaps,
melting the wax sealings — one more time — burning my eyes,
until I am blind anew, allowing me to see for the first time, again,
the unseeable things, illuminated by the cancerous sun, the
annihilating sun, a future no longer protected, unsealed,
the end of times, a vision that causes me to rend my vestments,
rend my skinny jeans, rend my cotton T-shirt, my cardigan,
careful rending, focused, tearing the fabric in casual lines,
that speak of my casual
anguish, the measured suffering that comes from being a small
god with big problems, a casual god, a nine-to-five god,
a god that works weekends,
if required, career-minded — that kind of god; jealous, small-minded,
in it for himself, because I am younger than I seem, conscious,
not of fashion, but of not-fashion, aware that twenty's the new thirty
and thirty's the new fifty; I am time grown old, I am young and very,
very old and I am seeing the future for the first time, again, and it is
a vision of me, projecting and being projected, putting myself out there
via super high frequency radio waves, mobile broadband, broadcasting
from the tallest buildings —
the Shanghai Tower,
CTF Finance Centre,
The Empire State Building,
The Trump International Hotel and Tower —
to everyone, everywhere, all at once,
ever-vital, like a virus...

Then I saw them, the Four Horsemen,
I watched them live vicariously through me,
watched them watch me as I live vicariously through my
own lives, watched them watch me projecting myself, being projected
putting myself out there at the highest register, where even dogs are
deaf, 5.8 gigahertz, where sound is no longer sound, where dolphins

can't communicates and bats
can't hear themselves think,
where radar is useless and the fluids of the inner ear spin
counter-clockwise, disorientating, watched the horsemen dismount to
watch me live vicariously through my own lives, viciously,
watched them watch me learning, living, loving, projecting myself, being
projected, watched them watch me as I put myself out there and put
out in the bathhouses of America, in the public bathrooms of America,
put out in the bushes and backseats of America, the absent bedrooms of
America, watched them watch me go down on my knees and go
down, the carnal supplicant, counting my blessings, one blowjob
at a time, America; watched them watch me lick the salt from
the backs of your daughters, America, from the backs
of your sisters, your mother, America; watch me kiss each pretty one
as I bind their hands behind their backs, as I drag the cat-o-nine-tails
'cross their bosom and tell them that love has never tasted this good;
I am the salt in the water, I am the light in the moon and the sun,
subject and object, my own pornographer, projecting myself, the
image of the mirror, as the Horsemen
dismount and take stock:
Horseman One, who is Youth, the seven-headed serpent,
who looks but never sees, sees but never observes, who observes
but never remembers; he is taking stock.
Horseman Two, who is Competence, the blind aesthetic, peering
through me with black sockets, holding under one arm
a small dog that sniffs the air as her master advances without
moving, embraces without feeling; he is
embraced but never held, he is understood but never
explained, America, he is created but never contained; he is taking stock.
Horseman Three, Comfort, the emaciated virgin,
death grey, bulimic, who carries in one hand a plastic sceptre and
in the other, a worn down toothbrush, who shows me her brown smile
as her dry fingers scratch behind my ear; she is taking stock.
Horseman Four, who is Celebrity, who is void and without form, America,
who breeds without issue, who promises to call but never does; he is

taking stock.

I am the fifth Horseman and, like the god of the Jews, I have a name
that can't be uttered, and a visage, like the god of the rest of us,
that can never be looked upon, a compressed god with expanded
ambition, a serious god who gets it, who can laugh at himself, the Alpha
and the Omega and Everything in Between, a god vast and
unseen, because size matters but visibility doesn't, a god that takes
no shit, a jealous god, an unhappy god, the god of day-timers and missed
appointments, the god of receding hairlines and hormone
replacement therapy, the god of Viagra, the god of all sexual love, the
god of reality television and all things in this and every
America: I am time grown
old, creating world destruction; you shall take
no other gods before me, because I am a jealous god and
vengeful and you must live
vicariously through me, as I live
vicariously through you,
one small lie at a time...

I am dazzled by the sun, America, as it rises, countless pixels,
I am strapped to the ground by the opulent sun as it
scrapes across the morning sky,
pinning me like a butterfly to a cardboard mat,
the arrogant sun,
casting shadows across the Book for the End of Times
until the wax sealings, melted, slide to the ground and the book
opens for the first time, a book but not a
book, a book that can be held, but is not held, a book that
can be read, but is not read, a book that can reveal, but conceals,
this is the Book of the End of Times,
a story with no beginning, America, just a middle with an end,
a story that advances like a virus, through an exchange of fluid, from
one mouth to another, or through casual contact with unwashed hands,
a story that is writ as we live it, a story that tells the secret
of the End of Times, the worst kept secret, because

we are living it at every moment and have
always lived it; it is a story with no message or moral, a
cautionary tale that urges you to repent, but knows you
won't because these are now and have always been the End of Times,
and we are small gods with large intestines, we have a taste for
everything and a capacity for love that is only exceeded by our capacity
to ignore the obvious.

The books says:
there will be drought, but the waters will rise,
there will be feast, yet the young will starve and eat themselves,
there will be laughter and music, yet there will be no joy,
there will be light in the darkness, yet the light will be cold and
the darkness will never be truly dark,
there will be righteous men, yet they will do wrong,
there will be trumpets, yet they will herald nothing,
there will be wisdom and false wisdom, yet they will be one and the same,
fires will scorch the earth, yet nothing will burn,
there will be medicine, yet the people will grow sick,
there will be peace, yet only in the name of war,
and there will be men of peace, who will murder for their cause,
and there will be plenty in the midst of nothing,
and nothing in the midst of plenty,
and the greatest among you shall be the least by far,
and the least among you shall be less than nothing,
and twenty will be the new fifty and fifty the new thirty and thirty
the new dead.
The books says:
Seven Armies will rise on the Seven Continents
and at the head of each army, Seven Princes holding Seven Swords
surrounded by Seven Generals astride Seven Horses
and the armies shall advance and not advance, moving forward and
retreating as calm as glaciers; then on a herald's signal, unheard,
the armies will disperse, the Seven Princes will disperse, taking with
them the Seven Swords, and the Seven Generals will disperse,

astride the Seven Horses
and the Seven Battles will rage, America,
everywhere at once,
in the shopping malls and gallerias,
the show homes and used car lots, in doctor's waiting rooms
and in schoolyards, in renovated townhomes and homeless shelters
and houses on either side of any street, in Walmart washrooms and Costco
checkout lines, the International Food
Courts of the nation and fitting rooms of Old Navys and Baby Gaps
and American Eagle Outfitters; the enemy will advance and retreat,
disguised as friends or as strangers, sisters — mingling, drawing
you into conversation with questions about your health,
your family, everyone smiling, everyone concealing themselves,
everyone a quiet perfect lie, personalized terrorists;
there will be men of peace who will kill for their cause,
there will be plenty in the midst of nothing,
the greatest among you shall be the least by far,
and the least among you shall be less than nothing,
because I am time grown old,
because I am young and very, very old,
because I have set things in motion,
because I am not the Redeemer,
because I have come to annihilate worlds,
because these are the End of Times:
don't worry, you'll get used to it...

And the hungry will eat dry soil and lick at the wounds around them,
and the thirsty will drink fire and taste terrible fire that will scorch
the universe
and the holiest will sleep naked in the beds of temptation
and fire will rain down from the Heavens
and ye shall thirst
and there will be no Righteous
only Clean and Unclean
projecting Themselves, being projected, America,

putting Themselves out there via
super high frequency radio waves,
mobile broadband, broadcasting from
the tallest buildings —
the Jin Mao Tower,
the Guangzhou International Finance Centre,
the Great Ziggurat of Babylon —
to everyone, everywhere, all at once,
persistent, like glaciers, innocent, like a child burning ants with a
magnifying glass, each of us our own Horseman, each of us an
image of an image of an image,
each of us, singing a song to ourselves,
celebrating ourselves,
each of us, singing muted songs of lamentation,
singing atonal dirges,
too slow and vastly modern,
inscrutable songs with no discernible melody,
each of us, singing ourselves to sleep,
singing a hymn to sleep,
as we live vicariously through our own lives,
small gods of infinite dominion, learning, living, loving,
reaching our vast hands out to adjust the stars:
they are too bright,
there are too many of them,
they are too close,
the arrogant stars,
the selfish stars;
you can hear them almost singing
when you close your eyes at night.

Death Sonnet

You've spoiled me for love, Death, taken from me
by the yard what I had earned by the inch.
You came as Beauty, Death; the Jasmine stench
lingered on my skin. How lovely you seem'd
tugging at my belt. You twisted slowly,
Death; I heard you creep along the fringes
of our bed, felt you crawl across her skin.
When I turned on the light I'd see only
your shadows. I blamed myself: I didn't think
I could hold love, the dreadful cage within
me would not unlock. I did not know, Death,
you were already there, lying beside
me, your hard fingers caressing my thigh,
your dry lips drawing closer for a kiss.

Leda and the Swan

It isn't Zeus, that horny cob, who breaks her with
his improbable lust, but it's downy thunder
just the same. A random uncle's cloacal kiss,
tendered with aviate still, holds her under

the watery night; she stops her breath and counts
to infinity. Zeus he is though, a hungry,
fickle intemperance, who comes as her aunties
drink away the day; she enumerates each stair.

Hist'ry's headway didn't erode, no Agamemnon
dies, no poets write no feath'ry lines about feath'ry
hands upon her ivr'y thighs; just Leda, deep,
and a withering uncle who shivers then leaves
to pour rum-and-cokes then drift to his cold bed

as she wipes the penna from her lips, tries to sleep.

Epiphany at the Grave of Patrick Lane

We shouldn't have buried you, Patrick, you weren't
ready; parts of you — the heart, the brain — were still
working, your pen still flowed.

Sometimes we're too hasty to make an end,
too ready to mourn; we wanted to miss you,
take stock, celebrate.

We mistook your clear eyes and embalmed liver —
it seemed the undertaker had already come and
done his work.

We had to bury someone, Patrick; you were
the right length and heft, it hurt our backs to
lift you, but we got used to it.

You'll have to stay planted, Patrick; the plot, the
headstone, we paid cash. Death provides
no refunds.

Besides, you could use the rest, and know better than
most that it's much easier to resurrect the living than to
unencumber the dead.

The Last Northern White Rhino is Dying

Drought skin parched, cracked as California mud,
parched as Africa mud, a thirsty river
bed, a dry lake absent of vegetation,
withered wedge, single black eye the only moisture.

Armored haunch, dry as a Saigon martini,
the last male northern white rhino flicks its tale,
lifts the treasured nub, draws unnecessary breath
the guard adjusts his rifle, watches his back.

Each uncertain step counted, every shit a
matter of record, casting dim eyes for
water, ignorant of his impotence; head bent
to graze; near-sighted, he cannot see the future.

Face of fat Sudan famine, cartographic folds
won't adapt, won't evolve, won't release the phantom
horn, treasured decay, keratin and calcium,
fallow stump, hangover cure for Hanoi tycoons

the guard draws rough fingers across the plated
rump, tracks a thick crease, pats the desolate haunch,
nuzzles against the pleated maw, whispers into
that unlikely ear, the tail snaps; insects scatter.

Poachers steep on invisible edge, we hold our breath:
protect the small brain behind the wet eye, protect the
still raw stump, protect the thirsty skin stretch'd over
bone strong as ivory; escort this thought into extinction.

Elegy

For Jess

You were not so big that I couldn't hold you
nor so small that I didn't hear your footsteps on my backstairs.
You wrapped me in your love,
that disconcerted mantle,
and positioned me in that narcissist gaze
that brightened me in your own reflection,
a love more infinite than sorrow,
more timeless than the moment between when you came
and when she left,
a love more focused than a coffin,
more generous than a pimp,
a love abstract as water,
more concrete than a Dextromethorphan high,
sweeter than a cocaine kiss,
calmer than codeine sleep,
soft as rain on heroin lips,
a speedball love, that seduces with everything it's got
then leaves you half-naked on a couch to worry and shiver;
an accumulation of bad choices — that kind of love
disconcerted, perfect.

I thought of you as a child, I only ever did,
not because you were innocent, you were never guilty of that,
not because you were fragile, your anger couldn't be broken,
but because you were uncertain, like a child, and terrifying,
and while never seeking this approval, you needed it at every turn.
When I let you grow, or rather,
let myself grow up despite you,
I gave up on you, piece by piece — we all did —
until, in turn, you gave up on you.

And when you died you left me hating
the parts of you you could not kill,
and hung me on the memory of our last embrace
when you said, "I love you" and I said,
"I love you, too."
Only when I turned to go did I see the mirror behind:
I still don't know if you were talking to me
or to your reflection.

The Poem of the Future

will radiate outwards in all directions at
once, no longer linear expression, but
centrifugal like kids on a merry-
go-round, or another simile,
as yet unimaginable,
commonplace in the future;
it will be written in
dead languages like
Akkadian
Coptic and
English;
words
being
instantly
translated and
transmitted; while they're
not necessarily
appreciated by all
people in all places at all
times, they're readily available
to all people in all places at all
times, and universally admired by
those beloved critics and their armies of readers.

Will be assembled, not crafted, by collectives
of children, chained to their desks, in those countries
still poor, using words sourced from emerging
nations and rhyme schemes yet undevised,
created by vast computers,
with artistic flourishes
added by grad students,
strictly supervised,

then polished by
editor-monks.
Poets,
like
today,
will not be
poets at all,
but serious men
in serious suits, men
who will make sure that poems are
taken seriously: like poems
today, but more so. Just the journals
will stay the same; they'll still take three to five
months to respond; and while the praise will be scant,
even rejection letters will come with a cheque.

lament for the ghost of carlos montenegro

the phone is drunk
calling people at
random: unapologetic.

it's night and the
phone has been on a
bender since thursday. the ghost

of carlos montenegro
is on hold waiting for an old
girlfriend to pick up. the ghost

of carlos montenegro,
as real as any memory
(a pebble in your heart that

hurts when you walk
or try to love again) is waiting
for its ex to pick up.

in life, it walked with
the zapatistas and ho chi minh
was lover to eva perón

and all three gabor
sisters; in death it
is a memory on hold.

"never question
the reality
of carlos montenegro's ghost,"

paul said the night
before he died. "and never
question the reality of

the phone company;
they are all that stand between us
and the darkness."

Future Tops of America

for Joey

The country salutes you,
Future Tops of America,
the Joint Chiefs of Staff have
reviewed the agenda and like
what they see. The President
signed an Executive Order;
there'll be a pancake breakfast
on the steps of the Lincoln
Memorial, and in every burgh
and borough — from Loring Park
to Key West, mayors have
commissioned gold keys, to
unlock those ancient hearts, as
good people — neighbours and
friends — stand on tippy toes to
catch a glimpse of this mighty
army of men and angels.
Everywhere, across the nation,
people are waiting to see what
you do next. Onward — unhurt,
unhated — like Christian soldiers,
marching as to war...

The route is set,
Future Tops of America,
for a ticker-tape parade, up
Chartres Street and down Orange
Avenue, across the West Side
Highway to the very end of
the Centerville Turnpike, past the
white-washed ranchers with

Huck Finn fences, past the tire
swing hung from the old oak tree,
festooned now with pink and
yellow ribbons, past the little
brick chapel, still wet with
Sunday prayers, past the junior
high, where the marching band
practices show tunes from the
approved list, where a solitary
boy lays in the cold, uncut grass,
dreaming of tetherball and a
Valentine kiss. Onward, little
brother, child soldier for this
fabulous Crusade, marching as to
war, but not as to war, as to
something even better...

Moms are baking,
Future Tops of America,
on every kitchen sill, from
Winnepago County to Wahneta,
apple pie and rhubarb Brown
Betty and every manner of
cobbler, crisp and crumble are
cooling in the afternoon shade.
Reverend Larson's organized a
box social in the park —
everyone's invited — and later
there's a potluck by the
Kenduskeag bridge. The Warren
boy will be there, Scotty Weaver,
Steven Charles, their bellies full
of bumbleberry coffee cake and
whoopee pie, buttermilk biscuit

and Tollhouse cookie. As the
bonfire fades, you'll assemble in
the town square to renew the
glorious stomp, marching, ever-
forward, because when you
stand, you stand alone...

Everyone's joining in,
Future Tops of America,
faster than a hidden glance; you
can feel the shift from Seattle to
Central Park, from Montrose to
Greenwich Village and all along
the Appalachian Trail. Domino's
is focus-testing toys for the
Junior Daddy JoyBox kid's meal,
batteries not included, as Carl's
Jr. launches the Future Tops
Bases Loaded Breakfast Burger:
three eggs — one sunny side up,
one over easy, one completely
scrambled — wedged with a slab
of lean sausage between two
pieces of dry toast. The
Salvation Army called, Future
Tops of America; they love the
whole marching motif, it's
something they can really get
behind: a single force, fresh-
faced, steadfast, fueled by
brotherhood and *amyl nitrite*,
ready to get down to business,
but never too busy to cuddle.
Even the Boy Scouts are getting

into the act, with patches for
Transgender Studies and Edging,
Voguing and Water Sports;
you'll be prepared for anything in
the America of the future, Future
Tops of America. Onward
Rebecca Wight, unhurt, unhated,
as to war or something better!
Onward Roxanne Ellis, unhurt,
unhated, as to war or something
better! Onward Eddie Justice,
unhurt, unhated, as to war or
something better! They are lining
the streets, brothers and sisters,
waiting for you to pass, like Christian
soldiers, marching as to war, but
not to war. As to something even
bigger than war, something even
smaller than peace...

Jesus loves you,
Future Tops of America.
It's not a gay thing, He loves you
as a person and thinks next time
He's in town you should Netflix
and chill. In church halls and
chapels across America, from
Roanoke to Grant Town to
Laramie, in mosques and
synagogues, from Fayetteville
and Topeka, in Kingdom Halls
and Christian Science Reading
Rooms, in Shinto shrines and
even every ashram, ordinary

folk, from Coconut Creek to
Braxton, are on their knees,
praying: God speed, Future
Tops of America! Concerned
women are no longer
concerned, abiding truths have
given way to intemperate joy.
General Hollis sent a heart-
shaped balloon, a dozen yellow
roses and a handwritten note —
"Love is not a sin, no matter how
fleeting; crowns and thrones may
perish, kingdoms rise and wane,
but we shall never falter" — as
everywhere, across the nation,
good people, God-fearing men
and women, are answering the
call. Andy Gipson walks with
you, Future Tops of America,
John McTernan and Charles
Worley — Onward! — a single
force, one body, one mind,
steadfast but never settled,
because when we stand, we stand
alone, but when we march, we
march together...

There's a rhythm,
Future Tops of America,
a kind of music that masks the
crack of thunder and that distant
hiss; it's hypnotic, the thump of
the boot, the thump of pump.
You would dance if you could,

Future Tops of America — the
Hustle and the Funky Chicken,
Do-Si-Do and Grind — but the
music is inside you now, and
every heart beats as one, because
you are marching with angels,
treading where only saints have
gone before, steadfast, determined,
the ranks increasing geometrically,
faster than a lover's cry, faster than
a mother's heart can break, your
ranks are growing and growing.
Spread the word Ricky Rius, let
the syllables explode from your
lips at 2,500 feet-a-second! Spread
the word Simmie Williams, unhurt,
unhated! Spread the word, August
Provost and hold your head high
because everywhere, good
Americans — mothers, fathers,
sisters, brothers — are lining this
and every street, waiting — quietly,
patiently — for you to pass.
Onward Brandon Teena, unhurt,
unhated, marching as to war or
something better! Onward Jason
Mattison, unhurt, unhated,
marching as to war or something
better! Onward Daniel Fetty,
unhurt, unhated, as to war or
something better! Onward Paul
Broussard! Onward Nireah
Johnson! Ever onward, Future
Tops of America, marching as to

93

war, but not as to war! As to
peace, but not as to peace! As
to something greater than war!
Something greater than peace!
Something not-quite formed and as-
yet unnamed, something very
nearly glorious, the kind of
something that, in this moment —
as the crowd stands in silence,
watching you pass — looks an
awful lot like love...

Closure

We gave ourselves the lesser years, and what
they lacked in abundance we made up for
in the comfort of each other's skin. When
we could not say goodbye or separate
those pieces of us still connected, we
shadowed each other until we became
ourselves shadows; though the end did not
come, but rather, came and went of its own
accord, I remember: there was no last
kiss; the singularity, conceived
in unmeasured moments, dissipated
a half-life at a time until there was
nothing left but distance and the hope that,
maybe, we could forgive ourselves.

About the Author

 Christopher Gudgeon is an author, poet and screenwriter. He's written eighteen books, from critically acclaimed fiction like *Song of Kosovo* and *Greetings from the Vodka Sea*, to celebrated biographies of folksinger Stan Rogers and iconic poet Milton Acorn. In his varied and spotty career, Gudgeon has worked as a psychiatric orderly, rent boy, bartender, rock drummer, TV weatherman, bible salesman, radio sportscaster and rodeo clown. He lives in British Columbia and Los Angeles. Follow him on Facebook and subscribe to his @1millionmonkies Twitter feed and YouTube channel.